Praying the Gospels through Poetry: Lent to Easter

PEGGY ROSENTHAL

ST. ANTHONY MESSENGER PRESS

Cincinnati, Ohio

Nihil Obstat: Rev. Richard W. Walling
         Rev. Hilarion Kistner, O.F.M.

Imprimi Potest: Rev. Fred Link, O.F.M.
         Provincial

Imprimatur: + Most Rev. Carl K. Moeddel
         Vicar General and Auxiliary Bishop
         Archdiocese of Cincinnati
         September 24, 2001

The *nihil obstat* and *imprimatur* are a declaration that a book is considered to be free from doctrinal or moral error. It is not implied that those who have granted the *nihil obstat* and *imprimatur* agree with the contents, opinions or statements expressed.

Scripture quotations are from the *New Revised Standard Version Bible*, copyright ©1989 by the Division of Christian Education of the National Council of the Churches of Christ in the U.S.A. Used by permission. All rights reserved.

Other permissions to reprint previously published material may be found on page 86.

Cover and book design by Constance Wolfer

ISBN 0-86716-422-0

     Library of Congress Cataloging-in-Publication Data

Rosenthal, Peggy.
  Praying the Gospels through poetry : Lent to Easter / Peggy Rosenthal.

    p. cm.
Includes bibliographical references and index.
  ISBN 0-86716-422-0
  1. Christian poetry, American. 2. Easter--Poetry. 3. Lent--Poetry.
I. Title.
  PS3618.O8435 P73 2002
  811'.54--dc21

                  2001004715

Published by St. Anthony Messenger Press
www.AmericanCatholic.org

Printed in the U.S.A.

Contents

Preface

> ...let faith be loud
> With the best imagining we have.
>
> —*Elizabeth Jennings*, "Act of the Imagination"

Sometimes we find that the best-loved Gospel stories
become so familiar that we can no longer respond to them.
Poetry's special art is to cast a fresh eye on the too familiar.
Poets are contemplatives, for whom the word is the vehicle
of the soul's awakening. When their meditation is explicitly
on a Gospel passage, word meets Word in new ways of seeing
and knowing. *Praying the Gospels through Poetry* presents one
poem for each chosen Gospel episode and reflects on the
poem so as to bring it into dialogue with the Gospel and
to invite the reader into the exchange. I hope that this
procedure will offer poetry as a fresh way to enter the
Gospels and pray with them more fully.

    For this volume covering Lent to Easter, I've chosen—
from the Roman Catholic lectionary—the Gospel readings
for Ash Wednesday, Holy Thursday, Good Friday and Easter
Sunday, along with the Year A Sunday Gospels for Lent.

I selected the Year A readings because they're an option each year for use with the Rite of Christian Initiation of Adults (RCIA) and so are heard most frequently in Catholic parishes. Protestant readers are likely to hear all these Gospel texts as well, since the *Revised Common Lectionary* used in many Protestant churches is based on the Roman Catholic lectionary. (The only difference that affects this book is that some Protestant churches celebrate Transfiguration Sunday as the Sunday before Ash Wednesday, transferring to that Sunday the Catholic lectionary readings for the Second Sunday of Lent.) My quotations from the Scriptures use the *New Revised Standard Version*.

The poems I've chosen are, with one exception, by contemporary writers: poems written in the past few decades. I favor contemporary poems because they speak directly to our situation, and because there is a wealth of outstanding spiritual verse being written that I'm eager to introduce readers to. (The one exception is a seventeenth-century poem that is such a profound meditation on the Gospel that I can't resist sharing it.) Some of the poems reflect explicitly on the given Gospel episode; some engage the Gospel tangentially. But all—and this has been my main criterion in selecting them—are ones that reward frequent readings. They are poems that I myself keep wanting to return to because each reading leads me somewhere unexpected, poems that continue to surprise me with an illumination of life's mystery, without treating that mystery as a puzzle they've solved once and for all.

Each Gospel unit in the book follows the same format. First, the chosen Gospel is indicated by Scripture citation.

The passage isn't printed; I assume that readers will refer to their own Bible. Instead, I offer a summary of the Gospel, highlighting features that will be reflected on through the poetry. The summary ends with the following transitional line, repeated in each unit:

Let's enter the scene with the poets.

The chosen poem is then printed, followed by an invitation to pause over it. I don't want readers to rush on into my own comments on the poem; in fact, I don't want readers to rush at all. One of poetry's great gifts is to slow us down. We're used to racing ahead as we read, whether it's a newspaper or an e-mail memo or even an essay: language in these forms propels us forward, urging us to grab up its main points. But poetry doesn't press ahead so much as hold us still—in the wonder of words crafted to open into another dimension. "What distinguishes poetry from ordinary speech," said Russian poet Osip Mandelstam, "is that it rouses us and shakes us awake in the middle of a word. Then the word turns out to be far longer than we thought." I want you, the reader, to feel comfortable remaining a while in poetry's lengthening words, so each poem is followed by a meditative mandala and the suggestion:

Let's pause and sit with the poem before going further;
reread it more slowly, let it sink in.

Then follows what I think of as my stroll through the poem. Poet A. R. Ammons has suggested a delightful metaphor: "A poem is a walk," he says. So I stroll along with the poem on its walk, inviting the reader to join me in my reflective ramble. Where the poem enters the Gospel episode, the reader is invited into the interchange between Gospel and poem. My goal is to offer guidance while also leaving imaginative space for the reader to move in other directions as well.

Next is a section introduced by the phrase *Now I wonder*.... I list three or four wonderings that the poem has stirred up in me: perhaps something about the poem's craft, or its insight into the Gospel, or its bearing on my own life; perhaps something about other poems treating this Gospel episode, or about how reading poetry can be a form of prayer. My hope is that these wonderings will open up still more reflective space for you, the reader, to stretch out into wonderings of your own.

Finally, there is the invitation to make the poem your own by memorizing a bit of it that especially speaks to you. Years ago, in the first course I taught on poetry and spirituality, one of the participants—Joan, a retired engineer—delighted us each week by reciting from memory a poem we'd been studying. She told us that whenever she met a new poem, her question about it was: "Would I want to memorize it?" This was how she judged whether a poem would be a good prayer resource for her; it had to be meaty enough for her to want to work at incorporating it into her mental storehouse to have on hand (or on mind) for continued spiritual nourishment. We don't all have Joan's talent for memorizing whole poems! But we can all commit to memory a line or two—and be much the richer for it. A line that I've made my own can be my mantra for the day or the week: As I drive to work or wait to check out at the supermarket, I can silently repeat the line, letting it act as prayer.

So here are some poems to accompany you through the special moments of Lent that the church offers us in these deservedly beloved Gospel readings. Lent blesses us with a time to pause in a special way…to linger over the wisdom of these treasured texts and let them gradually form us anew in Christ. Lingering with poetry in this long, graced pause can enrich not only these Lenten days but also our Easter experience. Poet Andrew Hudgins, in a poem called "Two Ember Days in Alabama," ponders how Lent's pause can look barren even while it is swelling in mysterious ways. Watching blackbirds "peck through dried-up winter weeds" to amass energy for their exodus north, then seeing them "simply leave," he muses on nature's rhythm become the rhythm of the supernatural:

> First fall, then winter. Then this long pause. And then the starting over. And then the never-ending.

Ash Wednesday

Almsgiving, Prayer and Fasting

Matthew 6:1-6, 16-18. We think of Ash Wednesday in terms of dust and ashes, and of the resolve to turn away from our sins, because these are the themes of the day's special liturgical rite. But the day's Gospel actually mentions none of these. The Gospel introduces us to Lent by focusing instead on the traditional Lenten practices of almsgiving, prayer and fasting. That we'll *do* these activities is taken for granted: Each section of the reading begins with "*Whenever* you give alms/pray/fast..." It's *how* we do them that is the Gospel's concern. We're firmly instructed to do them "in secret."

"Whenever you give alms/pray/fast," don't do it showily like hypocrites; "truly I tell you, they have received their reward." Three times we hear this warning, word for word, and three times we hear the positive command: "when you give alms/pray/fast," do it "in secret." Then at the end of each verse comes the refrain: "and your Father who sees in secret will reward you." With its repeated refrain and parallel phrasing, this Gospel feels very much like a poem. So it's natural to enter it anew by means of a poetic reflection.

Let's enter the scene with the poets.

from Love's Bitten Tongue

Lord, hush this ego as one stops a bell
Clanging, cupping it softly in the palm.
Should it make music, silence it as well,
For there's no difference when one wants calm
Of silence from the ego's loud tinnitus
Buzzing in spirit's ear with no relief,
With every reverence a false hiatus
Which brings those moments I name prayer to grief,
Tempts me to think I better honor them
By turning away from prayer as I did once.
So my thoughts, snared by their own strategem,
Like balls that children toss aside, all bounce
In my head back and forth until despair
Of praying may, in mercy, become prayer.

—*Vassar Miller*

*Let's pause and sit with the poem before going further;
reread it more slowly, let it sink in.*

"Lord." As I step into the poem, I step into prayer with this very first word: the poem is addressing God. With the next word, I know that it's petitionary prayer, a plea. "Lord, hush…"; it's a plea for quieting. And coming immediately next upon "this ego," I know it's *internal* quieting that I—or the "I" of the poem, the speaker—need.

She takes me then to a comparison: Her ego needs hushing like a bell, whose unpleasant "clanging" I'm hurled into without the chance to catch my breath, since no punctuation at the end of the line lets me pause. From "clanging" I step solidly onto "cupping": The repeated "c" ("clanging, cupping") cements the two words like adjacent matched pathstones. But suddenly something about their coupling makes me trip. I look down. Oh, I see: It's that they don't refer to the same subject. The *bell* is what's clanging, while the *person* (the "one") trying to stop it is "cupping it softly in the palm." The poet has chosen to throw me off balance a bit so that I'll jerk just as if I were grabbing to stop a clanging bell.

I move to line three. Even if the bell makes music instead of a clang, "silence it" is still the poet's plea. And beginning with the next line, I start to learn why. Music and clanging are equal annoyances when they come from the ego: that is, when they're "the ego's loud tinnitus," that distracting background noise of a constant "buzzing" in the ear. "Silence" from the ego's noise is what "one wants." That "silence": The poet brings me a second time to the word. A poet carefully chooses each word on a poem's walkway; so when she decides to repeat a word, I know it's important. She is setting it up as a signpost on the path, calling it to my attention.

"With every reverence a false hiatus...." The poem's path is stretching out along a lengthening sentence, as the poet extends her plea against the ego. Here, she leads me into her dashed hopes for a break from her ego's self-absorbed buzzing. Every hoped-for "hiatus"—every apparently reverent moment of prayer—turns out to be "false." Instead of "relief," the reverence that she longs to call prayer comes to "grief."

"Tempts me...." This sentence has gotten so long (I've now entered its seventh line!) that I need to stop and get my grammatical bearings. Stretching out the sentence through grammatical twists and turns, the poet crafts for me a frustration much like the experience she is describing, of being caught in the ego's snares. In a moment of panic, I wonder: *what* tempts me? The ego? The hiatus? Whatever it is, the temptation is clear—and dreadful: to "turn away from prayer" altogether, "as I did once." I sigh with relief that I've come to the end of the sentence. But it's an end that's no true relief, that's truly another grief, because it is the stopping of prayer. The poem's walk has taken me to what feels like a hopeless dead end.

I do go on, but into a thicket. My thoughts "snared by their own stratagem"—caught in the temptation to give up on prayer—hiss at me through those doubled "s"s like a snake. Then they "bounce in my head" like balls carelessly tossed aside by children, as if I'm trapped in a frantic play-space that takes over the space in my head. "Back and forth" my frantic thoughts bounce, until I come—at the end of the poem's next-to-last line—to "despair."

What saves me, however, is the absence of punctuation at the line's end. With nothing like a period or even a comma to hold me, I move without pause into the poem's final line, where I come, twice, to "prayer." Mercifully, prayer is forcing itself through all the obstacles against it. *Four* times, I now see, the poet has grabbed onto the word: Four signposts saying "prayer" have kept her going, and kept me going in hope along with her. And, yes, that's where the poem's final line finally brings me: to the hope that some-how, "in mercy," the very "despair of praying" may itself "become prayer."

And I recall that the poem has in fact all along been a prayer: a plea to the "Lord."

"Pray to your Father who is in secret," the Gospel instructs us. "Go into your room and shut the door." Pray alone in silence, not noisily for all to see. But what if the room of my soul is a racket? What if my ego is blaring like the hypocrites' trumpet in the streets? Praying (or giving alms or fasting) *in secret*—in the true hush of a humble self-effacing silence—is easier said than done. That's where the poem has led me: to see how challenging this Gospel's imperatives really are. Challenging because my own ego is the hypocrite that insists on calling attention to itself, whatever it does. When I give alms in order to get praise from others (or even just from myself), or when I call attention to my fasting, the ego has already, as the Gospel says, "received its reward": self-satisfaction.

The Gospel instructs us to quiet the ego; the poem dram-atizes what a struggle this can be. Yet falling in desperation onto God's mercy, the poem lands on the reward promised in the Gospel refrain: the secret meeting of my soul with God, which is true prayer. Lord, hush this ego, I pray.

Now I wonder…

- I wonder about the rhymes in the poem. The poem is a sonnet: fourteen lines rhyming in a pattern (here, a pattern of every other line rhyming, until the final two lines). Do any of the rhymes particularly catch my attention?

- I wonder about the poem's title. This poem is the first in a series of twenty-two linked sonnets, during which "Love's Bitten Tongue" eventually becomes Jesus silencing himself on the cross. In this opening sonnet, is the longed-for silencing of ego perhaps a form of biting my tongue?

- I wonder about how poetry in general might lead me to my God "who is in secret." Poets are experts on the inner life: They explore the hidden places of our soul. "Poetry leads us to the unstructured sources of our beings, to the unknown," wrote poet A. R. Ammons; "poetry is a verbal means to a non-verbal source. It is a motion to no-motion, to the still point of contemplation and deep realization."[1] At that still point, does God await me "in secret"?

- And I wonder about that "motion to no-motion" that poetry is. Poetry's motion is never a rush, never a race or even a power walk. It's a stroll like my favorite Sunday afternoon activity: a walk with my husband in the woods, along a well-marked path, with time to poke into the side paths, to gaze at the leaves, or just to sit. I need this ramble to quiet the pace of weekday life; I need poetry for

the same reason. If I do without either for too long,
I don't do well.

Returning to read the poem one more time...
is there a line or so that I want to memorize, to make my own?

First Sunday of Lent
The Temptation

Matthew 4:1-11. Good confronting the power of Evil. The tension is classic. Evil is determined to win control of the Good, by insinuating itself into the Good's very goodness, which Evil scorns as weakness. By tempting the Good to betray itself.

The Gospel gives voice to the classic confrontation. Voice and names: Jesus versus Satan. And the Gospel places the combatants in a classic structure: three tests or trials, as in folk tales the world over. Three has the archetypal meaning of completeness: If you can overcome three different obstacles, you can overcome anything.

These classic dimensions of the Gospel's Temptation narrative make it compelling, no matter how often we hear it. But we're compelled as well by another dimension, another tension: How (we can't help but wonder) do the temptations apply to ourselves? Where does Satan speak to us today? How does his voice sound? What exactly does he say to lure us into betraying our better selves?

Poets can take us into this dimension of the story because they are dramatists, in a sense. They invent voices. They set scenes. Or, in the case of a classic mini-drama like this one of Jesus' Temptation in the Desert, they reset it on a contemporary stage. Here is a resetting of Satan's third temptation: offering Jesus "all the kingdoms of the world and their splendor."

Let's enter the scene with the poets.

Matthew 4:8-11

"It's not much, I know, what with slums and the
     dubious types
who eat at the better tables. Still one can whine
forever, can't one? Take what comes when it's ripe,
I say. Pleasure's no evil if taken as a sign
that life is good. There IS an ease one finds
in this place: the limited joys that come with largess.
I've come to like it, a shock, perhaps from a mind
once filled with higher saws. Welcome... to 'The Best
We Can Do.' Allow me to pour you a middling sherry.
The decanter is chipped, but the maids are lively,
     can laugh.
And, if you allow, performers will keep us merry.
I'll call for a tweedler, one who knows his craft."
"You serve yourself at table, eat your tail,
while my quiet lovers reach, even now for the nails."

—*David Craig*

Let's pause and sit with the poem before going further;
reread it more slowly, let it sink in.

Oh dear—strolling into *this* poem puts me instantly in
Satan's company. Right into his voice, into his words to
Jesus as the poet reinvents them. I'm definitely not relaxed
with this walking companion; he has something unctuous
and ingratiating about him. While the Gospel's Satan had
a certain grandeur, proudly displaying the world's splendors
to Jesus, this modern Satan equivocates. He's showing me
worldly goods which he knows are a bit shabby but which
he's trying to sell me nonetheless.

Yes, I know the poet is having Satan direct his temptation
at me personally, at all of us who live the comfortable middle-
class life offered by our society today. And I know the poet's
Satan is tempting us to fall; that's Satan's business, of course.
So I listen warily as Satan plies his wares.

He wants me, from the start, to settle for second best:
That's clear. He's upfront about offering mediocrity, which he
tries to pawn off as a virtue: It's neither the extreme of slums
nor of wealth, he concedes, neither true poverty nor true
riches. But why waste time whining, he shrugs; take what
life offers and enjoy it. The "ease" of our modern desert of
abundance, the "limited joys" in our wasteland of "largess":
Hey, they're OK, he smugly laughs. Take *me*, his seductive

strategy continues. If *I*—who once tempted with grandly cutting maxims (the poet puns with "saws," letting it mean both a saying and a sharp tool)—can settle for lesser temptations, surely you can, too. "Welcome"!

"Welcome…" Satan has taken me, his cloying arm around my shoulder leading me on, to something he titles (with ironic, self-mocking pride) "The Best We Can Do." It seems to be the name of his party house, where his sleazy version of a good time is in full swing. Playing the role of the exaggeratedly warm host, he offers me "a middling sherry": middling like all the mediocrity he wants me to accept. "The decanter is chipped." What an apt image, I note with a shudder, of Satan's satisfaction with the less than perfect, of the tackily sharp edge he pours from today. He then promises me lively entertainment—promises me life *as* entertainment—but by "a tweedler." It's an old-fashioned word with creepy overtones: To "tweedle" is to play idly and carelessly on a high-pitched instrument like a fiddle; to tweedle is also to wheedle and cajole. So the tweedler's "craft" boasted of by Satan is a sly cajoling aimed at luring me to take life as a carefree entertainment, to sit back with a drink in my hands and an idle laugh, free of care for anyone else or for anything happening in the world outside this party house. "Loosen up! Join the party!" This is the gist of Satan's temptation.

With the word "craft," the poet ends Satan's crafty speech. Now that I'm released from Satan's grip, I have a chance to look back over his discourse. And beneath its slick surface, I'm startled to discover that it has been the first twelve lines of a sonnet. There indeed are the sonnet's standard five-beat lines and alternating rhyme pattern.

But the solid grounding of rhythm and rhyme that I expect from a sonnet has been utterly missing. The steadiness of the sonnet form has been hidden under—even distorted by—Satan's slippery gliding like a snake from line to line.

How different is this sonnet's closing couplet: the firm, deliberate rhythm of Jesus' measured response. The poet granted Satan twelve lines of the poem to make his sales pitch; here in a single couplet he has Jesus slap it down.

Jesus says in Matthew's Gospel: "Away with you, Satan! for it is written, 'Worship the Lord your God, and serve only him.'" Jesus elaborates in the poem: "You, Satan, serve only yourself." You are self-serving. Worse: You are self-consuming. While pretending to spread out food for others, you eat your own tail. A self-enclosed circle, you consume yourself "while my quiet lovers reach for the nails," calmly offering themselves for crucifixion if need be. My people—unlike you and your raucous consorts—are quiet of spirit. And they are true lovers: They *care* for one another and for all. They reach not for your complacent sherry but for the nails of self-sacrifice.

Jesus, too, will "serve himself," we know, but in a sense precisely the opposite of Satan's. Jesus will offer himself to us as the Lamb who is slain, serving himself to us for our salvation. In the noiseless crash of a couplet, the poet has Jesus turn the tables on Satan. And my mind flashes to another Gospel scene: I see the tables of the corrupt moneychangers in the temple being overturned by Jesus' righteous wrath.

Now I wonder…

- I wonder what "chipped decanters" I myself am tempted

to pour from...perhaps when I give of myself, but not wholly, holding back a bit in self-protectiveness?

• I wonder about the "ease" of our modern desert of abundance...shopping malls that pave over country fields, turning fertile land into blacktopped desert waste..."middling" moral values that are satisfied with a few hundred deaths by our nation's bombs as long as the dead aren't our own countrymen.

• I wonder about the claim of the poem's Satan that "pleasure's not evil if taken as a sign / that life is good." It's a seductively tempting statement. Life *is* good. So I wonder what's wrong with Satan's logic.

• And I wonder about the poem's dialogue format. It's rare for a poem to be entirely explicit dialogue, as this poem is. But every poem, even when it has no characters speaking in quotation marks, still dialogues with the reader. We walk through any poem in conversation with it; our reading of it animates it, gives it a listener and hence a voice. "The poet disappears into the poem, which stands mute," writes poet Edward Hirsch, "until the reader breathes life back into it. And only then does it shimmer again with imaginative presence."[1]

It shimmers in response to our engagement with it. A poem isn't monologue, it's dialogue: conversation between two. So a poem is incomplete until we join it, wander through it, wonder through it.

And when the poem is one whose content engages the Gospels, the conversation expands. Like a friend met

along the way of two others' Sunday walk, the reader is
invited to come along and share the exchange.

Returning to read the poem one more time…
is there a line or so that I want to memorize, to make my own?

Second Sunday of Lent
The Transfiguration

Matthew 17:1-9; Mark 9:2-10; Luke 9:28-36. It's surely a peak Gospel scene: Jesus dazzlingly transfigured on the mountaintop in company with two major figures of Israel's salvific history, with God's skyborne voice identifying for the disciples Jesus' unique role as "Beloved Son." The disciples would certainly have thought they were glimpsing heaven, since Moses and Elijah had long since been dead. Moses represented for them the "law," since he was considered to be author of the five biblical law books: God's commandments given to the Israelites not as arbitrary rules but as part of God's special covenant with them as chosen people. The law was gift, promise that if the people followed God's ways, God would remain with them and continue to care for them. Elijah, the Hebrew prophet taken up to heaven in a whirlwind at the end of his life, and believed to be coming to earth again to herald the Messiah, would have represented "prophecy." But prophecy in the Old Testament didn't so much foretell the future as pass judgment on how the Israelite community was going astray in the present. The prophets voiced God's threats of punishment if the people didn't correct their ways, but also promised God's ultimate mercy and healing.

What would Moses and Elijah—standing for the "law" and the "prophets," which Jesus' destiny was to fulfill—have been saying to Jesus when they suddenly appeared with him there on the mountaintop? The Transfiguration accounts of Matthew and Mark don't tell us. Only Luke suggests that they "were speaking of his departure"—that is, Jesus' death— "which he was about to accomplish at Jerusalem." Here's where the poet steps in.

Let's enter the scene with the poets.

from Transfiguration

> *And there appeared to them Elijah and Moses*
> *and they were talking to Jesus. —Mark 9:2*

They were talking to him about heaven, how all forms
    there were luciform,
How the leather girdle and the matted hair, how the lice
    coursing the skin
And the skin skinned alive, blaze with perfection,
    the vibrance of light.
And they were talking about the complexities of blood
    and lymph,
Each component crowding the vessels, the body and
    the antibody,
And they were talking about the lamp burning in
    the skull's niche,

The eyes drinking light from within and light from
        without,
And how simple it is to see the future, if you looked
        at it like the past,
And how the present belonged to the flesh and its
        density and darkness
And was hard to talk about. Before and after were
        easier. They talked about light.

. . . .

They were talking to him about law and how lawgiving
        should be
Like rainfall, a light rain falling all morning and mixing
        with dew—
A rain that passes through the spiderweb and penetrates
        the dirt clod
Without melting it, a persistent, suffusing shower,
        soaking clothes,
Making sweatshirts heavier, wool stink, and finding every
        hair's root on the scalp.
And that is when you hurled judgement into the crowd
        and watched them
Spook like cattle, reached in and stirred the turmoil
        faster, scarier.
And they were saying that, to save the best, many must be
        punished,
Including the best. And no one was exempt, as they
        explained it,
Not themselves, not him, or anyone he loved, anyone who
        loved him.

. . . .

I want to believe that he talked back to them, his radiant
    companions,
And I want to believe he said too much was being asked
    and too much promised.
I want to believe that that was why he shone in the eyes
    of his friends,
The witnesses looking on, because he spoke for them,
    because he loved them
And was embarrassed to learn how he and they were
    going to suffer.
I want to believe he resisted at that moment, when he
    appeared glorified,
Because he could not reconcile the contradictions
    and suspected
That love had a finite span and was merely the comfort
    of the lost.
I know he must have acceded to his duty, but I want
    to believe
He was transfigured by resistance, as he listened,
    and they talked.

—Mark Jarman

*Let's pause and sit with the poem before going further;
reread it more slowly, let it sink in.*

"They were talking to him about…" The poet enters the scene at a point where the Gospel writers give only a stage direction but no details. Reading in the Gospel that the disciples saw "Moses and Elijah, talking with Jesus," the poet wonders: Hmm, now that's a conversation worth imagining. And so he imagines it.

Imagining a biblical scene more fully than Scripture details it has a long and rich heritage. Our best term for it is *midrash*, the Hebrew name for the age-old practice of rabbis commenting on a biblical passage by responding to it imaginatively. "Midrash is both a serious religious and literary genre, and a form of wit,"[1] writes contemporary poet and anthologist David Curzon, who has also offered the insight that all poetry on the Scriptures is, in a sense, midrash. Certainly this is true for what poet Mark Jarman is doing with the Transfiguration scene. (He does it at greater length, I should note, than I've been able to reproduce here. The complete poem is seven stanzas; we're following him through the third, the fifth and the last.)

"They were talking to him about heaven." Here where we join the poet, he imagines that Moses and Elijah are telling Jesus their experience of heaven. They find it to be a place where everything physical is "luciform"—is transformed, that is, into light. But as they start describing this en-lightening process, what they actually get stuck on are images of the tough, densely physical stuff of fleshly existence that desperately needs heaven's transforming. The bodily trials of martyrs particularly get their attention. Starting with the surface discomfort of too-tight clothes, like a leather girdle (perhaps John the Baptist's), the poet pictures the speakers moving progressively deeper toward and into the flesh: down to the creepiness of "lice coursing the skin" and then the gory torment of martyrs' "skin skinned alive." He follows their imagined talk further right into the body, which from their heavenly view looks dark and cramped (though with an almost comic-book horror): crowded blood vessels where antibodies jostle for space; the claustrophobic "niche" of the skull.

The poet transmits all this imagined speech of Moses and Elijah in a deadpan voice, no matter how wild the images become. His long, expository lines and deliberately flat tone make Moses and Elijah sound like heaven's elders giving a schoolroom lesson to Jesus, who has lots to go through in the flesh (they hint) before he can get to the heavenly glories being promised him. Heaven's light *is* wholly transformative, Moses and Elijah assure him; it dissolves all that difficult bodily stuff of life in the present, making the future as "simple" to see as the past. The present, alas, is "hard" to talk about, they admit, because the present belongs "to the flesh and its density and darkness": to the clotted physical realm, to discomforts and even evils that are "hard" to face. Naturally, they'd rather talk about what's "easier," the "before and after"; so "they talked about light." But it's a heavenly light drunk by eyes that have seen in their earthly days the horrors of martyrdom such as those in store for Jesus. This is the light that they were talking about. We don't learn Jesus' response.

"They were talking to him about law...." And law starts off sounding unexpectedly pleasant, even "light" in its own way. It is like "a light rain" gently falling, so fine that it passes through a spiderweb without disturbing it. But gradually, almost imperceptibly, the rain's persistence gets uncomfortable, disturbing indeed: it soaks clothes, makes sweatshirts heavier, makes wool stink, until it is intrusively "finding every hair's root on the scalp," creepily penetrating to our physical core.

And then the poet suddenly makes us jump: "judgement" is "hurled" into the crowd, which recoils in terror. Is this the "fear" that the Gospel attributes to the disciples, a fear spread now by the poet to a crowd he imagines stirred up in panic at the mountain's base? And who is this "you" who has leapt into the poem to hurl judgment? Is it God, declaring Jesus as "my beloved Son" whose scary destiny—to take judgment into his own flesh—is being revealed?

From wherever the judgment has been hurled, it's as shockingly transformative as a lightning bolt. In the stanza's final three lines, the law that Jesus will embody gets spelled out. It is nothing less than the law of love, of sacrifice. Moses and Elijah lay it out with brutal clarity for Jesus: "To save the best, many must be punished," with no exemptions, not even for him "or anyone he loved" or "anyone who loved him." The law that began as light rainfall has become heavy, hard to take, unyielding, terrifying. This is the law that they were talking to him about. We don't learn Jesus' response.

Now, in the poem's closing stanza, we finally do: "I want to believe that he talked back to them." Jesus' response—or what the poet "wants to believe" that response was—is to "talk back" to Moses and Elijah, like a young person talking back in protest to parents who've presented a painfully unwelcome truth. Jesus flares up in resistance to what strikes him as life's harsh judgment, its unfair demands. It's as if Jesus has been listening, holding his tongue, all through the long speeches of Elijah and Moses, feeling his body consumed with righteous indignation (which to his friends looks like dazzling light) as he hears of the suffering to come for them all. *No!* the poet pictures Jesus objecting; *No!* It's too much, this law of redemptive love. Punishment for *anyone* who loves me, you say? An embarrassed blush at the thought of his dear followers' hard fate courses over his body: "that was why he shone in the eyes of his friends." What looks to his disciples like glorification is (as the poet tries to picture it) actually Jesus' all-consuming resistance to the necessity of the cross. He will "accede" to this necessity; the poet doesn't doubt Jesus' ultimate *yes* to love's painful law. But at this moment, imagining this scene on the mountaintop, the poet sees Jesus "transfigured by resistance, as he listened, and they talked."

"He was transfigured before them, and his face shone like the sun, and his clothes became dazzling white," Matthew's Gospel says, continuing: "Suddenly there appeared to them Moses and Elijah, talking with him." The very *content* of that talk is what the poem "Transfiguration" imagines as the *cause* of Jesus' appearing "transfigured before them."

Now I wonder…

- I wonder why the poet repeats the phrase "I want to believe" five times in the final stanza.

- I wonder whether the poet is deliberately envisioning Jesus' Transfiguration experience as if it were merged with his upcoming Gethsemane experience, that Agony in the Garden where Jesus prays that his cup might pass. Matthew's and Mark's Transfiguration episodes do lead right into Jesus' informing his disciples that "the Son of Man is about to suffer" and "be treated with contempt."

- I wonder about other people who have been transfigured by resistance to a difficult truth, set afire by a vision of the world's evil that they're being called on to combat in their very beings. Martin Luther King, for instance,…Oscar Romero,…people struck by the uncomfortable revelation of what it would take for the world's wrongs to be set right: the suffering of many, including the risk of their own martyrdom.

- And I wonder about another recent poem that pictures Jesus resisting the suffering inherent in the human condition, resisting out of solidarity with the humanity he has joined. Louise Erdrich's poem "The Savior" imagines that the newly incarnate Jesus, on discovering humanity's heavy lot in his own flesh, talks back defiantly to God the Father: "I hate the weight of earth / I hate the sound of water," that is, of humanity weeping its burdensome pain. Jesus vows to resist human suffering with all his divine being. "I will not stop burning," he declares, determined to burn the suffering away with his undying love.

Returning to read the poem one more time…
is there a line or so that I want to memorize, to make my own?

Third Sunday of Lent
The Samaritan Woman at the Well

John 4:5-42. She has come to draw water for her daily needs, this woman of Samaria. There by the village well she finds a Jewish stranger resting from his journey. He is thirsty but doesn't have a bucket to reach down to the water, which lies deep in the well. "Give me a drink," he requests of her, breaking Jewish custom not only by speaking with a woman but also by asking to share utensils with a non-Jewish person. The woman, bright and spunky, challenges him on both points. This sets going their lively dialogue that is the heart of the Gospel episode. He offers her a water that quenches one's thirst forever, the "living water" of "eternal life"; yes, please give it to me, she replies, so I don't have to keep coming to the well each day. He shifts ground, leaping into the core of her soul: You've had five husbands (had a life, that is, perhaps lacking restraint) and are now living with a man you're not married to. She sees that he has seen right into her. But instead of fearing his insight, she honors him as a prophet; and instead of judging her sinfulness, he honors her by revealing to her his identity as Christ.

The Gospel of John is poetry in a sense. It works, that is, through images that play against each other: pairing up, moving into opposition, toying with double meanings. So lively are this Gospel's images that they themselves sometimes seem to be the main actors in the narrative. In this encounter between Jesus and the Samaritan woman, their mutual requests for a drink mirror each other; the notion of "worship" is moved from a geographical place to the inner life of "spirit and truth"; literal food turns into "doing God's will"; literal water gushes up "to eternal life." So any poem enters John's Gospel as into a congenial medium.

Let's enter the scene with the poets.

Song of the Brightness of Water

From this depth—I came only to draw water
in a jug—so long ago, this brightness
still clings to my eyes—the perception I found,
and so much empty space, my own,
reflected in the well.

Yet it is good. I can never take all of you
into me. Stay then as a mirror in the well.
Leaves and flowers remain, and each astonished gaze
brings them down
to my eyes transfixed more by light
than by sorrow.

—*Karol Wojtyla (Pope John Paul II)*

Let's pause and sit with the poem before going further;
reread it more slowly, let it sink in.

Karol Wojtyla studied literature in college and was soon writing poems that appeared in Polish magazines. After his ordination to the priesthood, in his twenties, he continued publishing poetry. It is a quiet, contemplative poetry, often meditating on biblical moments. The encounter between Jesus and the Samaritan woman at the well particularly attracted him, so much so that he composed a sequence of eight poems reflecting on the scene. "Song of the Brightness of Water" is the last in the sequence, which was published when Wojtyla was thirty years old. So as I enter the poem, I'm joining not a pope but a young poet-priest.

And almost immediately—by the end of the first line—I see that I'm joining him in his persona as the Samaritan woman of the Gospel. She is evidently musing some time after the incident; her encounter with Jesus was "so long ago," she says. Yet she is still living it: The depth she experienced is "this" depth, very present to her now. And its brightness— "this" brightness—"still clings to my eyes."

From the poem's title I can tell that "this brightness" is the water's. Not until the end of the poem do I know for sure that the water's brightness is Christ's, his transforming light mirrored in the well as the woman gazed into the water. In a condensed, meditative poem like this one, my stroll through the poem can't follow a single straight path. It's more like the passage of my eye through a painting: all the images are before me at once, and I let my eye meander through their interrelations as the artist suggests them. What the poet suggests here is that the woman had met Jesus not only *at* the well but *in* the well: that throughout their dialogue, both were looking not directly at one another but into the well, meeting by means of their reflections mirrored in the water. His reflected depth had penetrated her being to become "the perception I found" as he revealed himself to her, and revealed her to herself in him.

The poet has deeply absorbed every word of the Gospel account, and assumes that we have, too, so that we'll know what this double revelation of Jesus consists in: Jesus revealing himself to the Samaritan woman as the Messiah who offers the water of eternal life, and revealing her to herself as a sinner who nevertheless is worthy of eternal life in him. Jesus sees into her soul and forgives what he sees, washing away her sin with his living water. For the poet, all of this astounding interchange of self-revelation and salvation is happening *in* the well itself. The well becomes the very image of the depths of self-perception that Jesus has drawn the woman into. This is "the perception" gratefully found by the poem's woman at the well.

But along with this perception, she says she also found her own "empty space" reflected in the well. I might think that finding empty space in myself could be a joyful relief, if I'm emptied of whatever clogs God's life in me. But the woman is evidently seeing the opposite sort of inner emptiness: a space that is empty now of Jesus, as she realizes that "I can never take all of you / into me." Their lives had truly merged at that moment in the well, mirroring one another as he absorbed her sinful being and suffused it with his own saving light; but human life can't *contain* Christ's fullness. We can meet Christ in the well, but then our human life in time inevitably moves on. The woman accepts this loss, this "sorrow" (accepts that "yet it is good"), because she knows that he will remain always available: "Stay then as a mirror in the well." There in the well, in life's depths, he will always be reflected when she comes to gaze on him. The light of Christ's dazzling brightness will always, now that she has once perceived it, transfix her eyes and transform her soul when she comes "to draw water."

Now I wonder...

- I wonder about the "leaves and flowers" that remain above the poem's well, brought down in the water's reflection by "each astonished gaze." Are they symbols of my new growth in Christ that is possible whenever I bring myself to gaze into his depths?

- I wonder about the very word "reflection," such a common word, reverberating through the poem. I've been reflecting on the Samaritan woman's reflections on her meeting Jesus' reflection in the well. A reflection is literally rays of light bending back from an object. When referring to the mind, a reflection is my thoughts bending back over an object, over a subject. Poetry tends to be reflective: to bend language back over its subject, taking my thoughts along and then loosing them to bend and turn again as they will, over the subject, over themselves.

- I wonder about the image of Jesus as "mirror." For Saint Clare of Assisi, "this image of the mirror is central," writes Murray Bodo, O.F.M.

  > As Francis was the mirror of Christ and Christ of the Father, so the life of the contemplative is to look into the mirror that is Christ and see there oneself, thereby learning who you are. By looking into the mirror who is Christ and recognizing yourself, you become a mirror of him whom you contemplate, and you in turn mirror, through Christ to the Father, all of creation. You see yourself both *in* a mirror and *as* a mirror. Saint Clare writes to her sisters: "For the Lord Himself has not only placed us as example and mirror for others, but also for our own sisters whom the Lord has called to our way of life, so that they in their turn will be mirror and example to those living in the world."[1]

  The Samaritan woman of the Gospel, model contemplative in the poem, does become an example to those living in the world: "Many Samaritans... believed in [Jesus] because of the woman's testimony," the Gospel says.

- And I wonder about poets as contemplatives. The American poet Sophie M. Starnes has said:

  > The poet lives in the contemplation of the individual moment. Such a contemplation requires...[that] the poet must become incarnate in one experience, dis-

tinct from all others. Through the isolation of one moment, the poet apprehends its heart and its edges, its thudding core and the fading wake of its sound. Only thus can the poet transfigure the experience, transcient as it is, into a living thing—into a poem that tremors out of a page into the heart of the reader.[2]

In "Song of the Brightness of Water," the poet— in the persona of the Samaritan woman—becomes incarnate in the experience of merging, for a moment, with God.

Returning to read the poem one more time…
is there a line or so that I want to memorize, to make my own?

Fourth Sunday of Lent
Healing of the Man Born Blind

John 9:1-41. This is the Gospel mini-drama of finger pointing. Everyone in the episode is accused by someone else of being a sinner. The man born blind, his parents, and Jesus are accused by the Pharisees; they, in turn, are accused by Jesus. And each accusation links sin somehow with blindness, the clearly symbolic blindness of not seeing truth even when it stands before your eyes. That Truth is Jesus, who gives sight to the blind man through the unlikely means of mud. It's the episode's most vivid moment: Jesus spitting into the dirt and smearing the mud with his own fingers on the man's unseeing eyes. Saliva and dirt—images of filth, dirtiness, mess, indeed of sin—become unexpectedly agents of light, of revelation. ("I am the light of the world," Jesus says just before making the mud; this man's blindness is "so that God's works might be revealed in him.") But there's another essential step to the process of revelation: The man himself must do his part, must share with Jesus the cleansing work. Jesus sends him to the pool named "Sent," to wash off the mud.

Let's enter the scene with the poets.

Sunday of the Blind

First a path made of clay,
then a path made of grass,
then a path of forget-me-nots
that runs straight to the sea.

My heart of shells.
My heart of flesh and blood.
My heart—a bruised star torn from your sky—
this is the one I bring to you, my God,
as a humble offering.

Your name is Truth,
your Word is love.
My Jesus, teach me the small truths like:
"I love you, mother!"
"I understand you, my son."
"I pray for you all."

When the small flower
sends her small truth
into the world
I don't think of the fallen cardinal
covered with a newspaper
or the fists that knocked my hair down
as if into a tomb,
or the hatred like a radioactive cloud
invading my past.

When all these truths disappear,
I lift my eyes to the cross
from which forgiveness comes.

and
I learn to forgive,
I learn to help the blind
how to see again love.

I was moving through the dust of years
when on the Sunday of the Blind
I looked for my soul and could not see it.
I began to pray

and You cleaned all the mud
with which I have covered my body
and gave me back
my eyes.

My prayer is hidden in this humble poem,
a tiny ladder toward You,
my Lord.

—Liliana Ursu

Let's pause and sit with the poem before going further;
reread it more slowly, let it sink in.

This poem doesn't enter the Gospel scene directly. First, it takes me on some introductory adventures.

I step into the poem on a path: "a path made of clay." But then right under my feet, the path is transformed...to grass,...then to forget-me-nots,...which lead—no, "run," *rush* eagerly—"straight to the sea." I pause and look back over the transformative experience that this opening, brief stanza has already brought me through: from lifeless clay earth, to the sprouting of hopeful grass, to the blossoming of delicate flowers whose name holds hidden memory, to the fullness of the wide sea's life-giving waters.

The next verse makes a leap: into the poet's interior, her very heart. Again, I'm led through a three-fold transformation. Her heart is, first, fragile shells (of the sea, I think); then it's her vulnerable flesh and blood; then it's—in a suddenly violent image that stuns me—a shocking image of cosmic pain: "a bruised star torn from your sky." In the single instant of that whiplash image, I'm hurled out into the heavens and yanked back into the woundedness of the poet's heart. And at this same instant, the poem becomes prayer: She offers her woundedness "to you, my God."

And I move on, into the poet's explicit prayer to Jesus. I hear irony in her praying for "small truths" which are hardly small, which are actually life's largest mysteries and longings: "love," "understanding," "prayer" itself. So the "small flower" sending "her small truth/ into the world" is an image of immense compacted power, all the miraculous power of love of the Little Flower, Saint Thérèse. With this power in mind, in her heart in hope, the poet can confront the alarming violences that her life has been attacked by. She doesn't tell us literally what these violent events are, because their literal particulars don't matter. What matters is how their violence struck her, so she presents it in metaphors that make vivid how violence kills. And these metaphors—of the fallen cardinal hidden by the surface happenings that pass for news, of fists knocking my hair as if into a tomb, of hatreds as insidiously invasive as a radioactive cloud—invite me to draw into them whatever violences have struck *me* (have struck anyone, everyone) in the same deadly way.

I stop, hold my breath, watch in horror, while these metaphors expand boundlessly, opening to welcome into themselves all the brutal hatreds that we inflict on one another, all the violence we commit, all the violence we are victims of.

Opening to our pain, just as Christ is open to our pain.

So naturally, my next movement is to "lift my eyes to the cross / from which forgiveness comes." And from there, I find myself in today's Gospel reading. The poet calls it "the Sunday of the Blind." She is *in* the Gospel episode, but sliding among its roles. Like the Pharisees, she has lost sight of her soul; but she also, like Jesus, "help[s] the blind / how to see again love." Like the blind man, she has her sight restored by Jesus through the unlikely means of mud; but she herself, rather than Jesus, puts the mud on her body (and on her whole body, not only her eyes); and Jesus himself cleans off her mud, rather than directing her to do it. But in both Gospel and poem, the blind person participates in the restorative process. And in both, the process requires Jesus' touch.

The poet's thanksgiving offering is "this humble poem" itself. From the "humble offering" of her violently wounded heart near the start of the poem, she has been able to move through forgiveness to a recovery. Touched by Jesus' healing, she offers her poem as "a tiny ladder" to reach him in her own way, the poet's way, the way of image and metaphor.

I glance upward from the final "my Lord," along the narrow lines' rungs, to the first "path" at the top. Yes, the poem is a ladder, a runged pathway, toward God: "toward You, / my Lord."

Now I wonder…

- I wonder about the deep suggestiveness of this poem, which moves entirely through metaphor: path, flower, mud, blindness. In his rich, delightful book called *How to Read a Poem and Fall in Love with Poetry*, poet Edward Hirsch reminds us that "poetry is made of metaphor." That is, "poetry evokes a language that moves beyond the literal."[1] By offering us language that's not fixed to a particular thing, a poet invites us to collaborate in making the poem's meaning. The poet of "Sunday of the Blind" doesn't want us to picture literal paths or mud, but rather to enter into the images with particulars of our own experience. We as readers help fill in the content of the metaphor, which always remains open to new connections brought by new readers.

- I wonder what mud Jesus is sending me to be cleansed of: uncomfortably messy family relations? work projects that sometimes drag me down? the violence of mud thrown at me? of unpleasant burdens I've placed on others? Whether or not the muddy situation is of my own making, how can I see Jesus' healing hand at work in the dirty, earthy stuff of life?

- I wonder about the linkage of sin and sight that's at the core of this Gospel episode. In the poem, the sins are left unnamed; instead, they are evoked as metaphorical violences...which helps me notice how, in the Gospel scene as well, no particular sins are pointed to. Rather, sinfulness itself is the condition at stake. And what a sharply terrifying image the poet offers for what sin does to us: "I looked for my soul and could not see it."

- And I wonder about the intimacy between poetry and prayer suggested in the poet's line: "My prayer is hidden in this humble poem." A poem can be a prayer, I know, even when the poet isn't explicitly addressing God. And a poem can be *like* prayer, sometimes, even when the poet isn't sure that God exists. Journalist Nora Gallagher intriguingly makes this connection in a brief episode in *Things Seen and Unseen*, her account of one year's life in her Episcopal parish. Recalling a conversation with her husband, Vincent, also a writer, but without her own habit of explicit religious practice, she writes:

> One afternoon, Vincent and I were driving home from the gym. "When I was writing a poem every morning, it took a lot of energy," Vincent said. "What I would call my writing energy. It cut it down. But now that I am not writing a poem every morning, I tend to forget who I am during the day. The least little thing blows me away."

> "That's exactly what it's like for me when I don't pray," I replied. "It is like a fragmentation. I fragment more easily."[2]

Returning to read the poem one more time...
is there a line or so that I want to memorize, to make my own?

Fifth Sunday of Lent
The Raising of Lazarus

John 11:1-45. From earliest Christianity, it has been
considered Jesus' crowning miracle. And for good reason.
The drama is gripping. Around the core figure of Jesus,
all the other characters are precisely delineated by their
reaction to him in this life-and-death situation: the
disciples, Martha, Mary, Lazarus, the ever-present crowd.
Jesus is not only the central actor but also stage director,
arranging events and speaking lines so that "they may
believe." Believe in what? In Jesus himself. He is, it turns
out, not only the drama's director and central character;
he is its very meaning, which is the conquest of death,
of all that binds us, buries us in the dark. His starkly
absolute self-defining statement can still give us chills
though we've heard it hundreds of times: "I am the
resurrection and the life." The movement of the drama
touches our deepest needs and longings. Death into life;
the bound let go; dark to light; from the cave, the glory
of God. And all taking place not only *through* but *in* the
person of Jesus.

Let's enter the scene with the poets.

Pietà

New Year's Eve, a party at my brother's.
Hats, favors, the whole shebang, as we waited
for one world to die into another.

And still it took three martinis before
she could bring herself to say it. How
the body of her grown son lay alone there

in the ward, just skin & bone, the nurses
masked & huddled in the doorway, afraid
to cross on over into a world no one seemed

to understand. This was a dozen years ago,
you have to understand, before the thing
her boy had became a household word.

Consider Martha. Consider Lazarus four days gone.
If only you had been here, she says, if only
you'd been here. And no one now to comfort her,

no one except this priest, she says, an old
friend who stood beside them through the dark
night of it all, a bull-like man, skin black

as the black he wore, the only one who seemed
willing to walk across death's threshold into
that room. And now, she says, when the death

was over, to see him lift her boy up, light as a baby
with the changes death had wrought, and cradle him
like that, then sing him on his way, a cross

between a lullaby & blues, mmm hmmm, while
the nurses, still not understanding what they saw,
stayed outside and watched them from the door.

—*Paul Mariani*

*Let's pause and sit with the poem before going further;
reread it more slowly, let it sink in.*

Poetry can lead us into the Gospel at an unexpected
angle.

First, it gives us a title. Here the title evokes the
much-loved tender image of the Holy Mother cradling
the dead Jesus on her lap. With this initial image, I'm
surprised to step into the poem at a New Year's Eve party.
What, I wonder, am I doing *here*, in this "whole shebang"?
When I reach the third line, I start to see a possible link:
Waiting for one world to die into another could be
pictured as the Pietà. But then I'm surprised again:
I come to a mother and her dying son, but not the pair
I'd expected. Nor am I any longer at the party, or only

at the party; I seem to have slipped into a hospital ward.

Then suddenly—"Consider Martha"—I'm in John's Gospel. The "she" of this stanza is Martha, rebuking Jesus: "Lord, if you had been here, my brother would not have died." But the "she" is also the poem's mother, saying to the poet at the party, if only you'd been here at the hospital twelve years ago when my son died.

But someone *was* there, I see: "this priest." He takes over as the acting subject of the poem's second half, just as Jesus does in the remainder of the Gospel episode. As Jesus, an "old friend" of the family, calls across into death to draw Lazarus "out" to life ("Lazarus, come out!"), the priest walks across death's threshold and lifts the boy up, "light as a baby," a being newly born. Truly, if the priest hadn't been there, the boy would have died, that is, been left as the "skin & bone," which is all that the fearful nurses could make of him. But because the priest cradled the boy and lullabied him, the woman's son didn't die but moved through death to birth. This is the mother's clear belief, as she recounts the event to the poet at the party where they're poised on the brink between two worlds. "This priest" is Jesus in the Lazarus miracle, transforming death to life.

This isn't the poem's only transformation. As I focus on the image of this priest cradling the young man and singing him on his way, singing "a cross / between a lullaby & blues," I can't help but see the Pietà of the poem's title. But—ah, the ultimate surprise—in this Pietà, it's the priest who has become the Holy Mother.

Yes, poetry can lead us into the Gospel at an unexpected angle. "Pietà" and the Gospel narrative of the Raising of

Lazarus intersect like two planes crossed at right angles. "Pietà" thrusts us into the exact middle of the Gospel narrative, and at precisely the midpoint of the poem. Then the poem continues *as* the Gospel story, told *as* the account of this priest ushering the woman's grown son through a death that is a birth, told *as* an image of the Pietà.

Poetry's gift is to give us this kind of layering, hovering, interpenetrating of stories, images, meanings. Through the poetry, the Gospel episode grows...expands into an unexpected present-day event. And as a reader, I grow through the poetry into dimensions of the Gospel's meaning I hadn't experienced before. Death in the poem, for instance, isn't an end but a process, a threshold, a passage into rebirth. Carrying this to the Gospel, I find the assurance that, yes, we are always living this continuum—as long as we live in the power of Christ. As long as we let Jesus call to us, "Lazarus, come out!" and heed his call, we can at any moment be reborn, unbound, renewed. This makes Jesus a midwife or mother, like the priest as the Pietà's Holy Mother. Through him, we are lullabied across death's threshold to new life.

The Raising of Lazarus is indeed Jesus' crowning miracle, but it wasn't a one-time event. It's as common as any birth, and as awesomely miraculous.

Now I wonder...

- I wonder about those three-line stanzas. Three is a key number for Christians—the Trinity. And I wonder why only three stanzas end with a period, the rest flowing into each other across the blank space that separates the stanzas.

- I wonder about the poem's and the Gospel's "dark": the black-skinned priest, Lazarus's tomb, the dark night of vigil through the boy's death.

- I wonder if I'd give this poem to a friend whose loved one has just died.

- And I wonder about all the "not understanding" in the poem. The nurses are huddled and fearfully baffled. They're the crowd watching the miracle of the dead man brought forth into life. But the crowd in this particular Gospel episode—in striking contrast to many Gospel crowds—*does* understand. They believe. I'm reminded of other recent poems on the Raising of Lazarus that focus on the crowd but turn it into a modern crowd that can't muster belief in what Jesus is doing:

There's "A Witness," by Spanish poet José Angel Valente. The poem retells the Lazarus story from the point of view of a modern person who, like all his neighbors gathered out of curiosity at the scene, has lost his spiritual sense perceptions and so can't perceive the miraculous nature of what Jesus is doing before their eyes. So when they seem to hear something like "Lazarus, come out," they all "go straight back"—into the grave of their ordinary lives.

The invented speaker in a poem by American poet Scott Cairns ("The Translation of Raimundo Luz: My Incredulity") insists that the so-called miracle is some sort of a trick; yet, despite himself, he reveals that Christ's life-and-death power does terrify him.

The crowd in another poem—"Lazarus," by New Zealand poet James K. Baxter—also stubbornly resists believing in God's transformative power, until Lazarus does in fact stumble from the cave into the sun's "furnace of rebirth," and then:

> What could they do but weep? infirm and humbled
> By Love not their love, more to be feared than wrath.

All these poets write out of a belief as firm as the Gospel author's. But they invent unbelieving responses to the Gospel episode in order to startle us into seeing what belief in this crowning miracle of Jesus actually entails. In the Gospel, it will entail Jesus' crucifixion: Precisely because many of the crowd "believed in Jesus" after witnessing the raising of Lazarus, the Pharisees feared that "everyone will believe in him, and the Romans will come and destroy both our holy place and our nations…. So from that day on they planned to put him to death."

So belief will entail his cross—

> a cross
> between a lullaby & blues, mmm hmmm.

Returning to read the poem one more time…
is there a line or so that I want to memorize, to make my own?

Passion (Palm) Sunday

Jesus' Triumph and Defeat

Matthew 21:1-11 and *Matthew 26:14—27:66*. This is the
only day of the church year when we hear two Gospel read-
ings at Mass. And what a contrast they are. The procession
Gospel narrates Jesus' triumphal entry into Jerusalem, with
the crowds laying out before him a royal carpet of palm
branches as they jubilantly cry, "Blessed is the one who comes
in the name of the Lord!" But soon the crowd is crying,
"Let him be crucified!"—in the Passion narrative which
begins with betrayal and ends with Jesus' death.

Experiencing the liturgy, we are torn between triumph and
defeat, adulation and betrayal, celebration and shock. There's
no day of the church year more fraught with tension. We sing
hosannas at one minute, shout "Crucify him!" at the next,
then fall silent as our Lord dies, humiliated, on the cross.

The clash of moods—the day's dense, tense complexity—
is encapsulated in the two names we have for it: Palm Sunday
and Passion Sunday. The church tries to pull together the
clashing experiences in the awkwardly combined name,
Passion (Palm) Sunday. Poets try by means of their own.

Let's enter the scene with the poets.

Palm Sunday

Three weeks ago forsythia rattled its sticks.
Now, though not an answer, not a reprieve,
The redbud flowers from its hard black trunk
And the magnolia rocks in the wind,

An ark that carries only whiteness and blush.
The dogwood's limbs have not revealed their bracts'
Stigmata, and for that she is thankful.
Why does He descend into the city,

She wonders each year, into History,
His advance raising up dust, a figure
Of dust, which is each of us following
Him? Dust the wind easily disperses?

And why do we repeat the meager fanfare,
The palm leaves bidding welcome and farewell?
She descends the church stairs and does what she must.
She hurries home to the life that's hers.

Each year she looks out for an answer and finds
Only spring's unmiraculous onslaught.

—*Eric Pankey*

*Let's pause and sit with the poem before going further;
reread it more slowly, let it sink in.*

The title grounds the poem in today's date on the church year's calendar. But *nature's* calendar is where the first lines place us.

"Three weeks ago" forsythia was in its winter state: no yellow blossoms yet, only bare branches. The forsythia "rattled its sticks," the poet says, as if the shrub were issuing a sinister warning. "Now" other early spring trees are blossoming—though not "answering" the rattle nor offering a "reprieve." Reprieve? The word jolts me, makes me wonder: reprieve from what? What danger or pain is lurking behind the lines here? I swing down to the next line for a hint—and find "the redbud" in flower.

The redbud trees in my neighborhood make me smile every spring, when their bright pink lacy flowers cluster along the length of the branches, looking like the frills of an overdecorated dress. But the poet won't let me see it that way. He stares right through the flowers to the "hard black trunk"—hammering in those three harsh words like nails.

"And the magnolia rocks in the wind..."

The magnolia trees in my neighborhood are so glorious, with their big bold flowers melding shades of pink and white, that I delightedly laugh out loud under their blossoms every spring. But the poet won't let me see it that way. He exudes disappointment, seeing "only" whiteness and blush, as if something essential and expected were lacking.

Then comes the "dogwood," spring's very sign. All over the eastern part of the country, flowering dogwoods brighten woods and parks with the delicate whites and pinks of their bracts, those petal-like features surrounding each small, hopefully green flower. But the poet won't let us see it that way. What he sees in the bracts—or what he anticipates seeing, for their time has not yet come—hits me as the ultimate shock of this series of grim images that have slapped spring's joy in the face. "Stigmata": the sign of crucifixion imprinted on spring's own sign of new life. The church's calendar is being pressed severely onto nature's in this poem.

But by whom? The very line that shocks me at its start with "stigmata," shocks me again with a "she": "and for that she is thankful." The poet has brought me, with one blow, to the brutal hammering of crucifixion over spring's hopes, and also to a new awareness of how I've gotten here. All along (it turns out) I've been in the consciousness of the poem's persona, a woman identified only as "she." So it hasn't been the poet himself who sees threat and disappointment and even the cross in spring's flowering trees. It has been his invented character: "she." It is "she" in whose mind, in whose company (I now realize), I'll continue through the poem.

To her mind, Christ's triumphal entry into Jerusalem, celebrated each year on this day, is somehow dismaying. She sees it as a "descent"—as if he plunges disruptively from above "into the city…into History." Why (the woman "wonders each year") does Christ do this? And as her mind's companion, I think: It's the very purpose of the Incarnation that she's wondering about, that she's challenging.

Christ's descent, in her mind, churns up "dust" and wonderings about dust, the word hounding her in three successive lines. She seems to be picturing, first, the literal dust that Jesus' colt would have raised from the dry dirt road into ancient Jerusalem. But this cloud of dust profoundly depresses her as it blows through her mind, turning everything into itself. She pictures the cloud of road dust enveloping Jesus, revealing him as no more than a mere "figure of dust," doomed to be dispersed by the wind. And "each of us following Him" is the same—or so the blur of her grammar suggests, blowing the "figure of dust" in two directions at once, back to refer to Christ and forward as "each of us following him."

I stand with her in the stanza, with all this dust of her anguished questioning swirling around me, all swept into her one huge churning question of "Why?" Why does Christ become mere dust, she agonizes; why does he descend into what we are, mere "dust the wind easily disperses"?

And as I stand there, letting the language of her questions whirl through my consciousness, I start to notice that the poet has subtly made all this dust carry even more significance. *Remember that you are dust and to dust you shall return*: the recollection of our Ash Wednesday rite, from the start of this Lenten season, echoes in the stanza's dust "which is each of us." But also borne in the language—in the artful wording of "His advance raising up dust"—is an anticipatory hint of the Resurrection that we'll celebrate one week from today.

Christ's Easter promise is that he will raise us up, "raise up" the dust that we are, transforming it into his own resurrected glory.

The poet implies that the woman herself, however, can't see this Easter hope that's hidden in her own language, swallowed up as she is in her despairing vision of dust. So although our annual Palm Sunday liturgy begins with jubilant celebration, she can't see it that way. To her, the palm-waving procession in church is a "meager fanfare," a yearly exercise in the futility of welcoming Jesus only to send him off to his death.

Naturally, then, she leaves the liturgy deeply dissatisfied. She "descends the church stairs," the poet tells us, and "hurries home." Her actions sound simple enough. But as I accompany her through them, I see that the poet narrates them with words carefully chosen to show me another dimension, a parallel story, that the woman doesn't see. She "descends," as Jesus himself was said to "descend" in stanza two. She "does what she must," as he did during his time in history. She "hurries home to the life that's hers," as Jesus will do in his Ascension: return home to the life that is his with the Father. That is, she is "following him" today, so that she can follow him next Sunday and beyond. The poet lets us see it this way, though he keeps the woman who is the poem's persona from noticing.

This narrative technique is called "dramatic irony": when the poet (or fiction writer) secretly gives us—through artful wording of the character's thoughts—an awareness that the character herself doesn't have.

So when I come to the poem's two closing lines, which

are a summary of the woman's yearly Palm Sunday experience, I'm poised in two distinct worlds of awareness. I'm in the mind of a woman for whom spring's hopes are only bitterly unfulfilled promises, who sees stigmata in the dogwood's bracts, who feels so threatened by spring's burst of blossoming new life that it strikes her as an "onslaught," an annual attack of the depressingly "unmiraculous." But I'm also in the mind of a poet who glimpses the word "miracle" hidden in the "unmiraculous," who whispers to me that the very "answer" which the woman "each year looks out for" is already *in* her ritual actions of the day. Palm Sunday gets her down, and the poet isn't trying to deny that emotional/ spiritual reality. He *hints* at the hope beyond it, but he doesn't force a facile joy.

Poetry isn't always meant to be consoling. As we enter Holy Week, it's appropriate to enter with a poem that shows us the day's threatening side. And truly, if I look at what today's Gospel readings give me, they offer no more of the Resurrection than the poem does. Jesus' triumphal entry into Jerusalem, in the procession Gospel, is followed by the Passion account, which ends with his death. So the poem makes me face questions that I'd rather not, but which are inherent in the day's Gospels: Where *am* I without the Resurrection? In spring's unmiraculous onslaught? Without the Resurrection, where is the very concept of miracle? What happens to my joy in each spring's glorious blossoming trees if the glory of God's resurrection promise is cut out? Without the church calendar's continuation from today into Easter, is nature's calendar left as an onslaught, an attack?

Now I wonder...

- I wonder about the poem's structure: four-line stanzas of iambic pentameter, the basic stately five-beat rhythm of formal English poetry. Counterpointed against this form, there's another structure of what seems three movements: The first movement, of seven lines, depicts nature's suffering; the second, of seven lines, is the woman's tense questions about the day's meaning; the final movement, of four lines, narrates her annual response. I wonder if the poem's meaning is manifested in this counterpoint of structures.

- I wonder about the dramatic irony of our annual experience of Passion Sunday. We live the liturgy in the light of Easter, though part of our consciousness deliberately blocks out the Easter promise so that we can experience also the day's potential for despair.

- I wonder about the most profound meditation I know of on dust: in Annie Dillard's book-length reflection, *For the Time Being.* Contemplating the nature of sand that blows over the earth's surface, Dillard (with her typically cosmic vision) sees successive epochs of humanity buried in layers of dirt. But she also, with the Jewish Hasidic mystics, sees each speck of dirt alive with God's fiery presence inside it. "Each clot of clay conceals a coal...A live spark heats a clay pot."[1]

- And I wonder about other ways that other poets have captured the tension of this day. I think especially of the sixth-century Byzantine poet Romanos, a deacon who wrote his homilies—amazing as this sounds—entirely as dramatic dialogues in verse. In his verse-homily for Palm Sunday, Romanos stretches taut the paradox of the King of Heaven choosing the poverty not only of flesh (in the Incarnation) but also of the lowliest beast to ride for his royal entrance into Jerusalem. The poet addresses Christ:

> You have shown Your strength in choosing the
>   humble, for it was a sign of poverty
> For You to sit on the ass; but as the Glorious One,
>   You shake all of Zion.
> The cloaks of the disciples pointed to frugality;
> But the song of the children and the throng of
>   people were a sign of Your strength,
> As they cry out, "Hosanna in the highest," a plea
>   to Save us!
> You who are on high, we pray, do save the
>   humbled!
> Heeding the palm branches, take pity on us,
> Look upon those who cry out:
> "You are the blessed One who come to call up
>   Adam."

The contemporary poet Anne Porter, in a poem called "Here on Earth," also plays with the paradox of Christ as the All-powerful God willingly reducing himself to our pain:

> He who has whittled
> A cabin for the snail

Has also carved our names
In the palm of his hand.

Here is Romanos's Glorious One who chooses our pover-
ty, the Creator who pierces his own palms to call us each
by name, suffering the stigmata which the persona of Eric
Pankey's "Palm Sunday" sees as the dogwood's bracts.

Returning to read the poem one more time...
is there a line or so that I want to memorize, to make my own?

Holy Thursday

Footwashing and the Last Supper

John 13:1-15. Every year the Gospel reading for Holy Thursday is the same: John's account of Jesus washing the feet of his disciples at the Last Supper. John's details, as always in his Gospel, are telling. In the middle of the meal, Jesus gets up from the table, takes off his outer robe and ties a towel around his waist; he pours water into a basin and begins the servant's work of washing the guests' feet. Peter—not understanding the deeper sense of what Jesus is doing—protests against his Master acting as servant. But Jesus insists, in language that resonates (like all of John's language) with symbolic meaning: "Unless I wash you, you have no share with me." And when Jesus is done, he points out the lesson: "If I, your Lord and Teacher, have washed your feet, you also ought to wash one another's feet. For I have set you an example, that you also should do as I have done to you."

"Do this in remembrance of me." Jesus also issues at the Last Supper this command which we honor on Holy Thursday as his institution of the Eucharist. We hear tonight, as the second reading, the most ancient description of the scene: Paul describing to the Corinthians how Jesus broke bread and said, "This is my body that is for you. Do this."

Jesus gives of himself *at* a meal, in the humble service of footwashing, and *as* a meal, in the Eucharist. And he does it all, John makes clear at the start, out of love: "Having loved his own who were in the world, he loved them to the end."

Let's enter the scene with the poets.

Love

Love bade me welcome; yet my soul drew back,
    Guilty of dust and sin.
But quick-eyed Love, observing me grow slack
    From my first entrance in,
Drew nearer to me, sweetly questioning,
    If I lacked anything.

"A guest," I answered, "worthy to be here."
    Love said, "You shall be he."
"I, the unkind, ungrateful? Ah, my dear,
    I cannot look on thee."
Love took my hand, and smiling did reply,
    "Who made the eyes but I?"

"Truth, Lord, but I have marred them; let my shame
    Go where it doth deserve."
"And know you not," says Love, "who bore the blame?"
    "My dear, then I will serve."
"You must sit down," says Love, "and taste my meat."
    So I did sit and eat.

—*George Herbert*

Let's pause and sit with the poem before going further;
reread it more slowly, let it sink in.

I don't want to give the false impression that George Herbert had Holy Thursday specifically in mind when he wrote this poem four centuries ago. The scene he invents is imaginary, is metaphor: Christ as the welcoming innkeeper who is Love. Yet for me, for years, this poem has been the perfect Holy Thursday meditation.

I meet Love, personified, in the very first word. Love warmly bids me welcome—to the poem, to the scene (whose setting I don't yet know). In response, my soul instinctively resists: No, I am not worthy to accept your welcome, "guilty of dust and sin" as I am. I "draw back," cringing in shame; Love "draws nearer to me, sweetly questioning" what I might need that keeps me from coming in.

I need a worthy guest in my place, I ruefully say. Love replies without missing a beat: That guest is you.

I, the unkind, ungrateful? No, impossible, I scoff. I am not worthy even to look into your eyes.

Love picks up my hand and my image in one gently smiling move: But I'm the one who made your eyes, you know.

Yes, but I'm the one who marred them, *you* know. My sin has ruined what you made. So I am not worthy to enter where you are. (By now, I see that it's a sort of inn, a refuge, and we're standing in the doorway.)

I keep resisting, insisting on my unworthiness. Love keeps resisting my resistance, insisting that he himself has already made good each fault I note.

Back and forth, our repartee goes—Love offering hospitality, I scrupulously refusing it—and all in the doorway of Love's dwelling. Love advances, I pull back. We're sparring with our wits, taking each other's words to turn to our own cause.

I shake my head dismayed. My shame, my shame.

But you know I've already taken on the blame.

Yes, yes, my dear (I feel tenderly toward Love, just unworthy). Well, then, all right (I sense myself starting to surrender). But if I accept your hospitality and enter, at least "then I will serve."

"Serve." My word is the last straw for Love. I've thrust at his heart, his very being. To serve is *Love*'s own essence, and he won't have *that* toyed with. He stands up tall and stops the playful cajoling with a final, absolutely firm imperative: "You *must* sit down and taste my meat."

Lord, I am not worthy to receive you, but only say the word. Silenced, I succumb to Love's command. I enter and let myself be served Love's very body, served by Love himself. I sit as guest at the eucharistic meal.

How have I gotten here, guilty of dust and sin as I still am? I look back over the course of the poem and see now how its pattern, reinforced by regular rhythm and rhyme, has been pulling me: Please come in...No, I am not worthy...*Please come in...No, I am not worthy...Please come in...No, I am not worthy*...COME! BE SERVED! EAT!

Come, be served, eat! This is what Jesus says to us in the
Holy Thursday readings. Love puts on his apron to serve us,
wraps a towel around his waist to wipe our feet. Peter
protests: "I, the unkind, ungrateful? You will never wash my
feet." But Jesus insists: "Know you not who bore the blame?
Unless I wash you, you have no share with me." It's almost
comical, how Jesus must force Peter to let himself be served
by God, how Jesus must force us to sit down and be fed by
his Body. He washes our feet clean of the dust and sin of
our human travels; he feeds us with his own meat. As Love
incarnate, he won't give up on us, won't stop giving of
himself for our good. Washed over with thankful wonder,
I sit and eat.

Now I wonder…

- I wonder at how *physical* Love is in the poem—drawing
  nearer to me, taking my hand, smiling right into my
  eyes—and in the Gospel, washing the disciples' feet with
  his own hands.

- I wonder about the poet's intimacy with us in this poem.
  He dramatizes a deeply personal experience of interacting
  with Christ, in metaphor that invites us into the most
  sacred place of his soul.

- I wonder about what I read in Robert Waldron's book
  Poetry as Prayer: Thomas Merton:

  > To penetrate the meaning of a poem requires that
  > we surrender ourselves to the poem. While reading

a poem, we can't be considering our vacation plans or thinking of our Christmas list at the same time. We must let go of life as we know it in order to enter into another's experience. We have to wear the poet's shoes, walk in the poet's footsteps. This requires humility. By entering the poet's experience we briefly give up our life in order to read and to meditate on another's life-rendering.[1]

...And entering another's life-rendering through meditation is taking a risk.

- And I wonder about the particular attraction and risk of surrendering to a poem that's *about* surrendering to Christ. Herbert's "Love" was the first poem I ever memorized as an adult. It was about twenty-five years ago, when I began to be drawn toward God and toward what would become (though I couldn't have guessed this at the time) my baptism in the Catholic Church. I'd been reading a biography of the twentieth-century philosopher/mystic Simone Weil, who called this very poem "the most beautiful poem in the world." She copied it out by hand, memorized it, and would recite it to herself with gripped attention, "thinking I was merely reciting a beautiful poem; but without my knowing it the recitation had the virtue of a prayer." Once when she was reciting it, during a period before she would have thought of herself as Christian, she experienced Christ's presence, "a presence more personal, more certain, and more real than that of a human being...an absolutely unexpected contact...a sudden possession of me by Christ."[2]

I memorized the poem, but with terror. Did I really want to experience Christ's presence? Did I really want to surrender to the poet's experience of surrendering utterly to Christ? I can't say that I've ever known Christ's presence as Weil did, as Herbert did. But I can't stop reciting the poem, out of love.

Returning to read the poem one more time…
is there a line or so that I want to memorize, to make my own?

Good Friday

The Passion and Death of Jesus

John 18:1—19:42. Who feels adequate to Good Friday? I
know I don't. Hearing the powerful, heart-wrenching Passion
narrative at church, I always feel overwhelmed by the mys-
tery of suffering. Every year it's as if I'm confronting the
painful mystery anew—as if I'm a child whose innocence
comes face to face for the first time with the evil of suffering.
Jesus' Passion and death are unique, I know, because they are
God's own experience. But as I listen to the Gospel account
of Jesus' pain and humiliation, I hear in it all the suffering
ever experienced in our broken world. How do we grasp it?
How do we respond adequately? Karl Rahner has written
that the Passion of Jesus takes place "not only in those
moments when the incomprehensibility of life can no longer
be denied, for example, when our dearest die, when a lifelong
love is forever destroyed by unfaithfulness," but also in the
apparently small losses and disappointments of everyday life.
But "this can be obscured both by the mysterious horror of
the cross itself and by the fact that we have become too
familiar with the language in which it is expressed."[1]

Here is where poetry can help. Poetry offers new language to enliven what has become over-familiar; poetry finds the unexpected word, the fresh image, that startlingly connects us to realities which otherwise elude our grasp. There are lots of recent poems that help me—if not to *grasp* Jesus' Passion—at least to *touch* something of its mystery for an instant. But I keep returning especially to this one by a contemporary Korean poet, I think because the Buddhist culture surrounding his Christian faith gives the poem just the unfamiliarity I need in order to connect with at least one point of the Passion narrative.

Let's enter the scene with the poets.

from Even the Knots on Quince Trees

A bridled,
foaming,
drooling
cow.

Aged four, my first revelation of really existing
found in a face like that printed by blood and sweat
on a cloth held out by a Jerusalem woman
to a man on his way to execution:
the face of a cow.

The yellow, twilit path slid up over a mountainside,
calligraphic in black and white,
I gazed at the face of the cow as it plodded along the
                                        muddy track,

and while I sat there perched on the leading cart
with an ancient cupboard roped down in the wagon

                                        behind,

my first buds of knowledge unfolded,
and I wept.

—*Ku Sang*

Let's pause and sit with the poem before going further;
reread it more slowly, let it sink in.

"Bridled." This is the first image the poem gives me: the
word stuck, solitary, friendless, in a line all alone. An image
of entrapment, imprisonment. Of victimization—for one is
bridled to be forced to do another's will.

"Foaming." Is this the foam of ocean surf, or of soap
bubbles? No, how could it be bubbly free, coming so close
upon that bridling? More likely it's the foam of forced effort
beyond endurance, or of helpless rage, the foam not of free
joy but of bound up sorrow, the body caught in a struggle
against desires not its own. Caught alone on the line.

"Drooling." An image of helpless humiliation, of the
body out of its own control. No one drools by choice. Babies
drool because they haven't yet gotten control of their bodies;
the old and the very sick drool when they've lost that control.

So, except in babies, drooling is an image of loss. And here
it is, lost and abandoned alone on the line.

"Cow." Now I have a concrete figure to attach to these
three sad descriptives. A living figure, a creature in bondage.
Bridled, foaming, drooling, she struggles along, alone on
the line.

"Aged four, my first revelation of really existing...." Now
I'm with the poet, as he recalls his childhood sight of this
suffering cow. He tells us that the sight was a revelatory
vision of his own self-existence—linked somehow to his
seeing the cow's face as like that of Jesus wiped by Veronica
as he trod his Way of the Cross. Not that at age four the poet
necessarily made all these conscious connections. But looking
back as an adult, he sees that he found his first conscious
self-image in the image of this cow whose face was the very
image of the suffering Jesus as imprinted on Veronica's cloth.

I can move further into the poet's vision here if I bring
along with me on the poem's pathway another poem,
"Station Six: Compassion" by Daniel Berrigan (from *Stations:
The Way of the Cross*), which pauses with Jesus at that
moment when:

a woman	Veronica	
(*vera ikon*	true image)	
removed her veil		
pressed it gently		
against that torment		
A gesture	spare	piercing
above all	consequential	
The cloth	drawn away	*eccolo!*

true image	*vera ikon*	impressed there
Who hearkens	who cares?	
her soul cries		
I must	I must...	
a mysterious	*quid pro quo*	
the afflicted one	*vera ikon*	cries out—
"I too am human!"		

As I walk the path—the *via dolorosa*—with these two poems, hand in hand, I see their hands reaching in concert to that compassionate touch of a tormented face, a touch which mysteriously grants a new level of existence to all involved: to Veronica, whose gesture of compassion imprints for all ages the "true image" of Jesus himself, his image held in her very name; to the sweat-foamed, bridled figure demeaned to a mere beast of burden, the afflicted one (his appearance "marred beyond human appearance," the Good Friday reading from Isaiah puts it) who receives the dignity of recognition in the gift of her touch; to the viewer, who like a child first confronting suffering with the eyes of compassion, senses himself forever changed by the sight.

Ku Sang continues his poem by filling in details of the scene surrounding his childhood revelation. It's as if his movie so far has been a close-up of faces, and now he pulls the camera back. As in an oriental painting, the setting is a steep mountainside, calligraphic, the vertical plane of its upward path suggesting the effort of ascent, while the yellow twilight casts a sense of the end of a long, hard day. Looking through the child's eyes, we stay focused on the face of the cow plodding upward through the mud. But now we also see where the child is seeing from: Sitting comfortably perched on the cart just ahead of the cow, riding backward, he takes into view the family's "ancient cupboard roped down in the wagon" which the bridled cow is dragging up the muddy mountainside track.

Taking all this in, "I gazed at the face of the cow..., my first buds of knowledge unfolded, / and I wept." Is the knowledge that makes the child weep perhaps in part his new consciousness of how the "ancient cupboard"—the ancient family heritage, the weight of the human family's accumulations from ages back—overburdens the poor cow who is bridled to it alone on the ropeline by which she drags it for them (for him, for us all) up the mountainside? Is it also perhaps the child's knowledge of his own comfort at that moment, "perched on the leading cart," a comfort that can however only be momentary, because he has already found his own identity (his "revelation of really existing") in the face of the bridled cow, seen as the image of the sweating face of God's incarnate Son on his Way of the Cross? Is it the heartbreaking knowledge that Karl Rahner articulates: "Have we never been terrified because the whole sorrow and torment of humankind seemed to confront us in a seemingly insignificant experience, in a tormented child, in a beggar or a dying person?"[2]—or in a bridled cow? "And did not this sorrow seem to invite us to recognize it as our own and to help to bear it, and to accept our own sorrow in such a way that all humankind's suffering would be more bearable and be redeemed?" If I answer yes, how can I not weep?

Now I wonder…

- I wonder about a phrase from a contemporary American poem on Jesus at Gethsemane called "The More Earnest Prayer of Christ," by Scott Cairns: "the divine in him contracted to an ache…." Is this another way of putting what Ku Sang's child saw in the face of "a man on his way to execution: the face of a cow"?

- I wonder about the poem's "gaze." The entire poem is the child's gazing: looking fixedly at a suffering face, taking it in. I wonder what happens when I *don't* gaze at a suffering face, when I pass by without looking, averting my eyes. Am I not then like the comfortable passersby in Daniel Berrigan's "Station Two: The Cross," those who single-mindedly, complacently, walk past a lone poverty-stricken man as he reaches deep into a garbage can:

> They lend not a glance   stride past…
> into a void
> past   that figure…
> faceless   nameless creature
> bending above   mere trash
> his mere life   trashed…
>
> Choose?
> refuse!

Do I choose to refuse to glance at the afflicted, my refusal turning them instantly into refuse (garbage, trash)? Do I render the poor "faceless"—deny their very identity, their existence—by "lending not a glance"? "Am I among those who pass by?" asks Rahner, musing on the meaning of our veneration of the cross; "am I in the procession that flows past the cross and spills into the darkness?"[3] Or do I have the courage of Ku Sang's child, to gaze at the drooling face of the poor creature plodding along life's muddy track?

- Or I wonder—since a gaze isn't necessarily for the good (if it's not a gaze of compassion)—whether I'm guilty of joining the "we" whom poet Andrew Hudgins pictures in his poem, "Ecce Homo," putting us into a Crucifixion painting by the Dutch artist Hieronymus Bosch:

> We glare at that bound, lashed,
> and bloody part of us that's Christ. We laugh,
>   we howl,
> we shout. *Give us Barabbas*,
> not knowing who Barabbas is, not caring.
> A thief? We'll take him anyway. A drunk?
> A murderer? Who cares? It's better him
> than this pale, ravaged thing, this god.
>   Bosch knows.
> …How easy evil is!

Like Ku Sang's child, Hudgins's "we" can identify with the bound creature: the "bloody part of us that's Christ." But Hudgins knows, with Bosch, that we're capable of the evil of scorning the sufferer with a mocking glare or dismissive shout. "Many pass by…," Rahner continues. "Perhaps they shake their heads, they laugh, they blaspheme." But "many remain… They kneel down… For as he was dying, the loneliest man of all"—lonely as the cow bridled in suffering flesh—"he knew them in the solitude of death and of abandonment by God. And he allowed all their bitter loneliness into his own heart."[4] Ku Sang's child is among those who remain; truly he is venerating the cross as he gazes at the face of the cow. But is one of his "first buds of knowledge," unfolding in his gaze, the same dreadful knowledge that Bosch and Hudgins and Rahner dare to face: that a gaze of scorn is possible, that he (I, we) are capable of glaring, laughing, at the bound and lashed? The ugly knowledge of "how easy evil is!"?

• And I wonder about whether I could look so clearly even at my own not looking, or face up to my sharing the evil of a mocking glare, without the aid of the poets. "It is a good thing," says Rahner,

> ...that we realize our condition only rarely, else we should not be able to bear it. But on this Good Friday we ought to consider of our own free will the terrors of life, so that we may stand fast when we must face the abyss and endure it. For we all are gathered round the cross of the crucified, whether we look up to him or try to look past him. We are standing under the cross, being ourselves delivered to death, imprisoned in guilt, disappointed, deficient in love, selfish and cowardly, suffering through ourselves, through others, through life itself, which we do not understand. Surely we ought to have the courage to let our heart be seized by God's

grace and to accept the scandal and absurdity of our inescapable situation as "the power of God and the wisdom of God" by looking up at the crucified and entering into the mystery of his death. [5]

Sometimes I need the poets to help me look.

Returning to read the poem one more time...
is there a line or so that I want to memorize, to make my own?

Easter Sunday

The Resurrection of Jesus

John 20:1-18. Of all the Gospel scenes of the risen Jesus,
the one that poets are by far the most attracted to is Christ's
appearance to Mary Magdalene in the garden. The Catholic
lectionary used in the United States cuts off the passage just
before this moment, so I've cited today's reading as given in
the Canadian Catholic lectionary and the *Revised Common
Lectionary* used in the United States and Canada, which
include the whole of this incomparably rich scene.

It's the first Easter moment that the Gospels give us: the
first appearance of the risen Christ to any of his followers.
Mary Magdalene is the one whom he chooses as the first
to hear and bear the good news.

She has come to the tomb before dawn and has
discovered it empty. She runs to get Peter and the Beloved
Disciple, returns with them to the tomb, then remains there,
disconsolate, after they've gone back home. Twice she is
asked, by beings beyond our earthly life, why she is weeping.
The second questioner, whom she thinks is the gardener, is
really Jesus, whom she recognizes the instant he calls her by

name. In her joy that he is alive, she naturally reaches to embrace him, but he restrains her. Instead of a hug, he gives her something infinitely better: the definite word of his risen life. And he sends her forth with instructions to the men back home: "Go to my brothers and say to them, 'I am ascending to my Father and your Father, to my God and your God.'"

Let's enter the scene with the poets.

Christ as a Gardener

The boxwoods planted in the park spell LIVE.
I never noticed it until they died.
Before, the entwined green had smudged the word
unreadable. And when they take their own advice
again—come spring, come Easter—no one will know
a word is buried in the leaves. I love the way
that Mary thought her resurrected Lord
a gardener. It wasn't just the broad-brimmed hat
and muddy robe that fooled her: he was *that* changed.
He looks across the unturned field, the riot
of unscythed grass, the smattering of wildflowers.
Before he can stop himself, he's on his knees.
He roots up stubborn weeds, pinches the suckers,
deciding order here—what lives, what dies,
and how. But it goes deeper even than that.
His hands burn and his bare feet smolder. He longs
to lie down inside the long, dew-moist furrows
and press his pierced side and his broken forehead

into the dirt. But he's already done it—
passed through one death and out the other side.
He laughs. He kicks his bright spade in the earth
and turns it over. Spring flashes by, then harvest.
Beneath his feet, seeds dance into the air.
They rise, and he, not noticing, ascends
on midair steppingstones of dandelion,
of milkweed, thistle, cattail, and goldenrod.

—*Andrew Hudgins*

Let's pause and sit with the poem before going further;
reread it more slowly, let it sink in.

The poem's title points me to a particular biblical scene:
the grounds just outside Jesus' tomb, where Mary Magdalene
sees a gardener working. But the garden I step into with the
poem's first line is clearly in another place and time. It's a
present-day park featuring a boxwood hedge pruned to shape
the four letters of a word: the imperative "Live!" With the
second line, the poet joins me, as if we're in the middle of a
casual conversation. "I never noticed it until they died," he
comments. So evidently (I take note) this is a park he visits
often, through the cycle of the seasons.

Stopping with the period at the end of the line, I smile,

noticing where the poet has cleverly brought me. In these two apparently simple, merely descriptive lines, he has actually drawn me into a death-and-life paradox: The boxwood's imperative to "live" isn't visible until its green leaves have "died" for winter. And as he elaborates the paradox over the next few lines, he subtly takes it (and takes me along) into its Christian dimension. "Easter" is the tip-off, of course. But there's also the "word buried in the leaves," the word "live," which I recognize as Jesus, the Word of Life, whose imperative to live becomes readable to us only through his death and burial.

In a burst of animation—"I love the way..."—the poet suddenly seems to shift the scene mid-line: "I love the way / that Mary thought her resurrected Lord / a gardener." But when I look back over how he slipped Easter images into his description of the boxwood's paradoxical movement between death and life, I see that there hasn't really been much of a shift. Right here in the park where we've been standing, the poet all along has been planting Jesus' surprise post-Resurrection appearance in the garden, "come spring, come Easter."

A more radical shift is with "He looks." That present tense instantly transports me into the present moment of the biblical scene. I'm there with Mary, seeing—as the poem's title announced—"Christ as a Gardener." But I'm seeing him through the eyes of a poet who "loves" imagining Jesus being "*that* changed." What might the resurrected Christ's first experience back on earth have been like if he saw *himself* as a Gardener? That's what the poet loves trying to picture. So he turns the poem over to Christ (to his imagination of Christ) in the role of divine gardener just returned from death to his land.

The field is untended, Christ immediately sees: "unturned," "unscythed," in "riot." And so, just as Christ did during his incarnated human life whenever he saw a need, he throws himself into meeting it. "Before he can stop himself, he's on his knees," tending to this wild, unruly field. "He roots up stubborn weeds, pinches the suckers": I can feel the feverish energy of Christ's labors, frantically digging into the dirt to create order out of our moral chaos. For *we* are the stubborn weeds, of course, and the suckers that need pinching off. The poet is playing with gardening language to generate metaphors for the risen Christ's salvific work among us.

"But it goes deeper even than that." I love the way the poet teases out a double meaning from that colloquial line. The "it" that goes deeper: It's simply the gardener's digging further down into the soil, but it's also (not so simply; painfully in fact) the Gardener's pushing his whole being further down into our stubborn, willful humanity, laboring to make right all our wrongs. "His hands burn" with the work; "his bare feet smolder." He's on fire with desire to give himself utterly to the work of ordering the field that we've let go wild. Or *still* on fire, I should say, since what he's experiencing is his recent Crucifixion, still fresh in his flesh.

The experience is exhausting him—so much so that "He longs / to lie down." I love the way the poet makes me feel Christ's aching physical yearning to be done with his sacrifice: nearly each word in the line is a "long" one, an accented one, so that the line drags heavily as I tread through it. "He <u>longs</u> / to <u>lie down in-side</u> the <u>long</u>, <u>dew</u>-

moist furrows." And to reinforce Christ's longing, the word "long" is repeated, referring now to the earth itself, which he is sinking into. The poet is imagining the risen Christ going through his Agony in the Garden all over again, this time after the fact of what had followed, after having drunk the cup that didn't pass.

But in the midst of his agony to die and be done with the pain of his pierced side and broken forehead, suddenly the poet's Christ realizes that "he's already done it"! He's already been through his Crucifixion and been raised: "passed through one death and out the other side"! He's so giddily relieved that "He laughs," and with a burst of joyous energy gets done his resurrection work in an instant: "He kicks his bright spade in the earth / and turns it over." I love the way that the poet, with joyous laughter of his own, takes that basic gardening act—turning over the earth with a spade in order to aerate and seed it—and makes it a metaphor for the salvific action of the Resurrection. The very earth, the whole world, is turned over, ready to receive new life. All our stubborn willfulness is overturned, turned under. We're given a fresh start.

The turned-over earth now jubilantly shares Christ's resurrection-freedom from toil and from time. In an instant, the seasons flash by. Seeds take on their own risen life and join the Easter dance, buoying Christ himself up for his Ascension. Then what a delightful closing image the poet brings us to: the wildflowers, which Christ had at first found an unruly smattering, now form themselves into stepping-stones for his ascent to heaven, so gracefully that he doesn't even notice what's happening. And we're left with that image, of the least valued of flowers—mere wildflowers (dandelion, milkweed, thistle, cattail, goldenrod)—transformed into the first bearers of Christ and now called by name.

"I love the way / that Mary thought her resurrected Lord / a gardener." Yes, the poet has shown us how much, and why, he does love Mary's vision. And I love the way that he loves it: the way the poet imagines Christ as a Gardener, turning the earth over at Easter.

Now I wonder…

- I wonder about the poem's iambic pentameter rhythm: that five-beat line that's English poetry's natural pace. *Because* it's the natural rhythm of our language, the poet can stroll into and through colloquial phrases unobtrusively: "Before he can stop himself…it goes deeper even that that…he's already done it." So the astounding events being described—Christ's death and resurrection and ascension—are disguised in casual attire. Like Christ appearing as a gardener?

- I wonder about how Christ's "not noticing" his Ascension (toward the end of the poem) takes me back to the poet's "never noticing" the word of life hidden in the hedge (at the poem's start). The Mexican poet Octavio Paz has said that "a poem is a spiral sequence that returns without ceasing—but without ever returning completely—to its beginning."[1] A poem can make itself a spiral through returning to certain words, or by picking up previous images, or through rhyme—through anything that loops me back to a point where the poem's pathway intersects with itself. But it's an intersection at a higher plane, since it opens for me a vista where I can look back over previous spots and see how they're linked.

- I wonder about the poem's final image, of the least valued flowers called by name as they're transformed into the first bearers of Christ. "Mary," Jesus said to her, "Go to my brothers and say to them, 'I am ascending to my Father and your Father, to my God and your God.'" Calling her by name, Christ transforms her (considered the least by the disciples, because she was a woman) into the first bearer of his risen word.

- And I wonder about why so many recent poets are drawn to this Gospel scene.

    For Kathleen Norris, in "Luke 14: A Commentary," the fun is in picturing how Christ pops up to surprise us in the most unexpectedly ordinary settings, how "he'll blend again into the scenery, and / more than once, be taken / for the gardener."

    For Vassar Miller, toward the end of "Love's Bitten Tongue," that amazing twenty-two sonnet poem dramatizing her struggle to break free from her ego's bonds, Mary's recognition of Jesus as he calls her by name is the key. The poet has been begging Christ for a way to emerge from "deep in the muck of myself," when she comes finally to the

    gray Easter day whose dawn will greet
    Your resurrection not seen by one eye…
    Till Magdalene comes dew-sodden and weary
    Being pierced open by Your whisper, "Mary."

And as Magdalene is "pierced open" at the instant of being called by name, the poet herself is painfully but blessedly "split open." Gaping with Mary at "Your gardener's clothes / Messy with muck and juices of bud and berry," she sees that if Jesus can be messy with muck, she herself can be, too, and in this acceptance of her ego she is paradoxically freed of its burden. The Gospel recognition scene has become for the poet a self-recognition, through seeing herself and Jesus remade as each other.

For Jorie Graham, in "Noli Me Tangere," the fascination of the scene is in Mary's reaching to touch Jesus and being rebuffed. This is the instant that has so attracted artists through the ages that it has its own name: the *Noli me tangere*, which is simply the Latin for Jesus' words to Mary, "Do not touch me." In long, swirling lines, Graham winds her mind through this famous moment when time and eternity long to merge but can't quite make it. And the poet herself wonders why Mary

must be driven back,
    why it is the whole darkness that belongs to her
and its days,
    why it is these hillsides she must become,
supporting even now the whole weight of the
        weightless...

Surprise, recognition, the transformative meeting of eternity and time. These are some dimensions of this marvelous Gospel scene that draw poets to it. "He was *that* changed," and so were we all. So *are* we all. The poets, moving their imaginations inside this earth-overturning change, help us muse on the wonder of Easter's gift.

Returning to read the poem one more time…
is there a line or so that I want to memorize, to make my own?

Notes

Ash Wednesday: *Almsgiving, Prayer and Fasting*

[1] A. R. Ammons, "A Poem is a Walk," *Epoch* 18 (Fall 1968), pp. 114-119.

First Sunday of Lent: *The Temptation*

[1] Edward Hirsch, *How to Read a Poem and Fall in Love with Poetry* (New York: Harcourt, 1999), p. 157.

Second Sunday of Lent: *The Transfiguration*

[1] David Curzon, *The Gospels in our Image* (New York: Harcourt Brace, 1995), p. xxix.

Third Sunday of Lent: *The Samaritan Woman at the Well*

[1] Murray Bodo, *The Way of St. Francis: The Challenge of Franciscan Spirituality for Everyone* (Cincinnati: St. Anthony Messenger Press, 1995), p. 29.

[2] Sophie M. Starnes, "Writing a Poem," *Christianity and the Arts* (Winter 2000).

Fourth Sunday of Lent: *The Man Born Blind*

[1] Edward Hirsch, *How to Read a Poem and Fall in Love with Poetry*, p. 13.

[2] Nora Gallagher, *Things Seen and Unseen* (New York: Knopf, 1998), p. 54.

Passion (Palm) Sunday: *Jesus' Triumph and Defeat*

[1] Annie Dillard, *For the Time Being* (New York: Knopf, 1999), p. 137.

Holy Thursday: *Footwashing and the Last Supper*

[1] Robert Waldron, *Poetry as Prayer: Thomas Merton* (Boston: Pauline Books & Media, 2000), p. 6.

[2] Simone Pétrement, *Simone Weil: A Life* (New York: Random House, 1976), p. 340.

Good Friday: *The Passion and Death of Jesus*

[1] Karl Rahner, *The Great Church Year* (New York: Crossroad, 1994), p. 142.

[2] Rahner, p. 141.

[3] Rahner, pp. 151-2.

[4] Rahner, pp. 151-2.

[5] Rahner, pp. 148-149.

Easter Sunday: *The Resurrection of Jesus*

[1] Octavio Paz, *Los hijos del limo* (Biblioteca de Bolsillo, 1987), p. 86 [author's translation].

Sources of Poems Quoted or Mentioned

Baxter, James K. "Lazarus." *Collected Poems*. Edited by J. E. Weir. New York: Oxford University Press, 1979.

Berrigan, Daniel. *Stations: The Way of the Cross*. San Francisco: Harper and Row, 1989.

Cairns, Scott. "The Translation of Raimundo Luz: My Incredulity." *The Translation of Babel*. Athens, Ga.: The University of Georgia Press, 1990; "The More Earnest Prayer of Christ." *Recovered Body*. New York: George Braziller, 1998.

Craig, David. "Matthew 4:8-11." *The Roof of Heaven*. Steubenville, Oh.: Franciscan University Press, 1998.

Erdrich, Louise. "The Savior." *Baptism of Desire*. New York: HarperCollins, 1990.

Graham, Jorie. "Noli Me Tangere." *The End of Beauty*. New York: Ecco Press, 1987.

Herbert, George. "Love." *The Temple*, 1633. In *Complete*

English Poems of George Herbert. Edited by John Tobin. New York: Penguin Books, 1992.

Hudgins, Andrew. "Two Ember Days in Alabama," "Ecce Homo," "Christ as a Gardener." *The Never-Ending*. New York: Houghton Mifflin, 1991.

Jarman, Mark. "Transfiguration." *Questions for Ecclesiastes*. Ashland, Ore.: Story Line Press, 1997.

Jennings, Elizabeth. "Act of the Imagination." *In the Meantime*. London: Carcanet Press, 1996.

Ku Sang. "Even the Knots on Quince Trees." *Wastelands of Fire*. Translated from the Korean by Brother Anthony of Taizé. Boston: Forest Books, 1990.

Mariani, Paul. "Pietà." *America*, January 2, 1999.

Miller, Vassar, "Love's Bitten Tongue." *If I Had Wheels or Love: Collected Poems*. Dallas, Tex.: Southern Methodist University Press, 1991.

Norris, Kathleen, "Luke 14: A Commentary." *Cross Currents*, Winter 1994-95.

Pankey, Eric. "Palm Sunday." *Apocrypha*. New York: Knopf, 1991.

Porter, Anne. "Here on Earth." *An Altogether Different Language*. Cambridge, Mass.: Zoland Books, 1994.

Romanos. "On the Entry into Jerusalem." *Kontakia of Romanos*. Adapted from the translation from the Greek by Marjorie Carpenter. Columbia, Mo.: University of Missouri Press, 1970.

Ursu, Liliana. "Sunday of the Blind." Translated from the Romanian by the poet (previously unpublished in English).

Valente, José Angel. "A Witness." *The Penguin Book of Spanish Verse*. Edited by J. M. Cohen. New York: Penguin Books, 1988.

Wojtyla, Karol. "Song of the Brightness of Water." *The Place Within: The Poetry of Pope John Paul II*. Translated from the Polish by Jerzy Peterkiewicz. New York: Random House, 1982.

We are grateful for permission to quote material printed by the following publishers:

Reprinted by permission of Franciscan University Press, "Matthew 48:11," from *The Roof of Heaven*, by David Craig, copyright ©1998. Reprinted by permission of America Press, "Pieta," by Paul Mariani, from *America* magazine, January 2, 1999, copyright ©2000 America Press, Inc. Reprinted by permission of the author, "Sunday of the Blind," by Liliana Ursu. Reprinted by permission of Story Line Press, "Transfiguration," from *Questions for Ecclesiastes*, by Mark Jarman, copyright ©1997. Reprinted by permission of Houghton Mifflin, "Christ as Gardener," from *The Never-Ending*, by Andrew Hudgins, copyright ©1991. Reprinted by permission of Alfred A. Knopf, "Palm Sunday," from *Apocrypha*, by Eric Pankey, copyright ©1991. Reprinted by permission of Random House, Inc. and the Random House Group. Ltd., "Song of the Brightness of Water," from *The Collected Poems of Karol Wojtyla/The Place Within*, by Karol Wojtyla, translated by Jerry Peterkiewicz, copyright ©1979, 1982 by Libreria Editrice Vaticana, Vatican City. Reprinted by permission of Harper and Row, "Station Two: The Cross" and "Station Six: Compassion," from *Stations: The Way of the Cross*, by Daniel Berrigan, copyright ©1989. Reprinted by permission of Crossroad, excerpts from Karl Rahner's *The Great Church Year*, copyright ©1994.